AF556969

The Devil's Radio

Jacob Rakovan

a division of

SMALL DOGGIES OMNIMEDIA

Portland, Oregon

SMALL DOGGIES PRESS
a division of Small Doggies Omnimedia
smalldoggiesomnimedia.com

The Devil's Radio
poetry by Jacob Rakovan

SMALL DOGGIES PRESS © 2013
1ST PRINTING.

ISBN 978-0-9848744-4-6

PRINTED IN THE UNITED STATES OF AMERICA
10 · 9 · 8 · 7 · 6 · 5 · 4 · 3 · 2 · 1

Small Doggies trade paperback edition, October 31, 2013

PUBLISHED BY SMALL DOGGIES PRESS, PORTLAND, OR.

Small Doggies Press: WWW.SMALLDOGGIESPRESS.COM
Jacob Rakovan: JACOB-RAKOVAN.BLOGSPOT.COM

Edited by ***Carrie Seitzinger*** & ***Matty Byloos***.
Cover Design by ***Matty Byloos***.
Cover Layout by ***Olivia Croom***.
Interior Layout by ***Olivia Croom***.
Type set in Celestia

The Devil's Radio

"The Demons sing with a raucous, trumpet-like voice"

—Nicholas Remy

Invocation

By water, by automotive collision, asleep and surrounded,
encircled by offspring by disease slow and steady,
by virtue of the bodies failure
the clockwork ground to halting,
in white rooms enlivened by florists,
by rouge and wax: by the concealed stitch in the lip
the cheap shoes, the rings removed and shared amongst the family
by slow degree, by pact, by violence
by the blossoming of strange flesh in the corridors of the body,
by cancer and by cancer and by cancer
by the failure of the heart
by slow and ponderous breath, by paralysis
each slow and honeyed day past savor
and the mouth gone down to dust,
to husk and shell by one's own hand,
by the million stratagems of a microscopic bestiary,
that devours us even as we live,
we are consumed, burning, dissolved in solution
in starlight, in the noonday sun
in privacy and in the public square.
We are discovered,
cleaned like a tagged buck,
hung by our heels to bleed,
stuffed with cotton and wax,
left to dry forgotten
in front of a television tube,
fallen down the bottle, the plate of powder.

This menagerie I have collected:
my clot of ghosts,
are one and all, natural as milk.

The Horrible Is Commonplace

Mercy Brown, fresh in the grave
was dragged into the light
a rabbit grabbed by the heels
and kicking.

She was a nineteen-year old farm girl
with galloping consumption
when, beside her mother and her sister
in Exeter Baptist churchyard, she was exhumed.
There was blood pooled wet in her heart.

Her mother was a husk of dry leather
and her sister, too, a discarded shoe in a wooden box
but Mercy was radiant in the dark
her cheeks, a hectic bloom.

For two months she had lain in the cold,
an unstruck match,
and Edwin, her brother, back from the dry climates to die
was sick and the family and the village gathered round
looking for a marvel.

Surely a bloodfat tick has drank poor George's family down.

So in March, when the ground was soft, they pulled her from the dark
and found her turned over, a restless sleeper
her liver filled with liquid blood and in 1892,
(the year that General Electric was founded,) they cut out her heart.
(In the year that Edison patented the two-way telegraph,)
they burned her heart to ashes.
They fed the ashes of her burnt heart to her brother.
Who died, regardless, two months later, leaving George Brown alone.

Later that year, a hidden lake burst from the side
of a mountain, killing two hundred holiday guests.
The city of St. Johns burned to the ground.

In Fall River, Massachusetts
Andrew Jackson and Abby Durfee Borden
were found, their heads burst like rotted pumpkins
side by side in the familial bed.

A Bedsheet Ghost

Your death, the mud bottomed lake
the half-stolen bikes jumped into it
warm water in a 4am hose.
Twenty-four beers in a cardboard flat.
Tar in the sun, liquid and black.
Each slow bubble is your death.
Here the man who drove us
to the center of the cornfield.
His cock, apologetic in his hand, is your death.
Here the beer can torn into a knife.
This also is your death,
on ripped brown vinyl seats
carried home on my back.
The stolen mail, the burning dumpster.

Oaks, scored with lightning.
Mushrooms and old papers.
The rags of your clothes,
your rotted camper, where you ran.
All the asylums and broken windows.
The liquor below your mother's sink
a dusty bottle of your death, beside the dish soap.
Your death a black telephone I call you on.
I throw gravel at the window of your death.
A white dog, a mirror full of blood, safety glass,
a blood-flecked lip, a lung, an empty balloon
a totaled car, a copper-jacketed bullet in your teeth.
Not you, the Polaroid in your casket.
Not you, the ash on the water.

There's a place where the tracks meet
where it is always almost morning.
The underpass and the gravel silver in a false dawn.
A field of fireflies and crickets and gas station wine
an electric hum, a wheat field, all that is left.

The River Is for Drowning Girls

Every song says it's true. Hair blooms in the cold current.
The little fish rise like angels to meet them.
They go down in the dark
in the good, black mud.
They roll, white-eyed through brown water.
Arms out in benediction.
Fish-pale bellies and breasts like a basement full of mushrooms
roots and blind things.

They say there are catfish big as Volkswagens near the dam,
that divers come up and never go down again.
They say when drought drops the water low enough
the old carved stones break the surface.

...and only say that you'll be mine
and in no other's arms entwine
down beside where the waters flow
down by the banks of the Ohio

Here, once, they humped the earth
like new dug graves in the shape of serpents
eggs, moons, wheels and bears.
Buried bones, copper axes, obsidian hands.
The river is for drowning girls.
Every song says it's true.

Train trestles cut across flat stones and mud
ring top beer cans, tangles of fishing line.
The river swells with rain and swallows fields.
Making mirrors of the mud.
Leaving fish to die for the corn.
Leaving the old stone blades of knives
arrowheads, bone beads and broken pots.

The river is for drowning girls;
hungry for them, it beats against the city walls
glutted with chicken coops, detergent bottles, syringes, empty jugs,
tampon applicators, slick black logs and fishing floats.

Dark as a rotted oak leaf
as a cold night, as the smoke
of a fall fire on the bank.
Dark as a barge filled
with west Virginia coal.
Electric light of a lone house
and a song ringing out:

...go down go down you Knoxville girl
with the dark and roving eye
go down go down you Knoxville girl
you'll never be my bride

The river is for drowning girls.
Girls drunk and dancing.
Girls fucking boys fresh
from jail, in cars.
In towns with cold smokestacks,
a blue line of crushed pills.

The river is for drowning girls.
They go down to the last line of land
and wait to be taken away.

Monee, Illinois Can Go to Hell

In the attic of a farmhouse
in the middle of rotting outbuildings
brown-eyed Susans, and
rusting lead-gas cars with dry-rotting upholstery
there is an upright piano
with an out of tune high C.
In the silence of that attic
are songs I carried on my back.
There are cats, that swarm
through the rusting tractors.
Through the crates of junk, the barrels
and cages and bones.
There is a red linoleum floor
where I am forever dropping
a puzzle piece out an open window.
Where I am stacking one chair atop another.

There is a stone I am flipping over
where the black ants are running
away with babies in their teeth.

In winter, the ghosts of pigs
stare through the greasy windows
at a black handled phone
still under my name.

(After *Child Ballad #44*)

I go, slow loping behind you
into sleep, you are a rabbit
and I all jack-scrambling hillbilly
hound, clumsy hurtle and slaver.

You have darted to the hills, to the tall grass.
The flushed birds rise and escape
the sour-grape hurtle of shot.

You are the slow doe trembling
at the edge of the wood.

I, the headlights scraping trees
A tangle of wire fencing.
I am the tree line of the hedgerow.
You, the pheasant eating the rich corn of dream
I, the badger among the mewling kits.
The dog loose with a rope and peg around his neck.

The Man Who Made the Nightingale

There are white berries in the ditch.
Thick husks of burrs hold stolen hair in strands.
A white birch stands in night soil.

There is a fairytale bridge.
Apple blossoms in spring.
A broken-down house with blue-green shingles.
A funny old man makes the children laugh and laugh.

He has an old black cat and a sad brown dog.
He has a mushroom ring and books
in black covers with pictures of machines.
He sings but the words are always wrong.

He has candy and new pocket-knives and string.
He has old wood and nails for building forts.
His house is full of secret places.
You can crawl right under it into the wet black dark.

He has the parts to a million bicycles.
He has lost kites and kittens and radios.
He has big white hands that flap at the end
of his long skinny arms and a round hairy belly like a barrel.
His owly eyes roll around behind thick greasy spectacles.
Sometimes if he hugs you too close you can see his yellow funny teeth
or smell his funny old smell.

His red kitchen is full of soft grey mice.
In the firelight, roasting hot dogs on sticks
you can see eyes like fireflies.
The gravel path from the door to the street shines in the dark.
The moon seems bigger over the funny old house.
It would like to tell you something, but has no tongue.

Ingrid Elizabeth Deardoff

Your pretty dress a hammer knocking against the eyes of God.
The sky is a stone. The tiny ants go about their blind business.
We have sown you, seed in the black soil of home.
Concrete angels feign weeping,
deathless and mute, they cannot curse.

Plastic flowers bloom and bleach in the sun.
The shining cars swarm on the black road.
Your name is stitched into our tongues
a synonym for grief,
should be a bird, a song, not coal or fire.

You cannot laugh.
We have washed your long-legged body,
the song of the saints goes on. How do they praise him for this?

O grinning death, you sonofabitch.
In the hills, in summer
tiny lights flit in the tall grass,
small stars under the trees.

Hilt's Law

The bones cast in the field like seed corn grow nothing,
grow briars in the boarded gas stations
brown stalks ready for the fire.
You do not hear our song,
earth thick in our throats, benzene, chromium
cadmium and arsenic
shuttered stores,
hosts of dead in cold-mill towns
the day that does not come though prayed for.

The trains of coal and corpses, the price of power
though wires are stretched like a mandolin on our backs
though the saints bob above us like car-lot balloons
You do not hear our singing.
In electric light the bubble gum machine is full of teeth
the babies' bottles with a slow sweet poison
the air thick with cancer, the rain with
teeth, without flowers, without cease.

This dream of sleep, in hunter's orange
over oil-black in cups, in the hollows under eyes.
The unborn sun in the darkest river, the hollow hills
unsong of un-place, Bloody Harlan, Centralia
the blessed fly over in air-conditioned comfort.

Let the bone-fire of your city burn 'till your shadow stains the bricks
Let the dark come spilling from the mine thick as molasses
Let the end come if it is coming,
Let the rich hang from their ankles,
a washtub full of black blood.
You do not hear.

Let the hills and stones fall on us and cover us
Let those curse us who curse the day, who are skillfull
the smelters of iron, and armaments, the hilltop removers.

Though we are dying, though we breathe black dust
and blue powder, spit liquor and blood
the black drink, the earth's secret breath.
Though we are toothless, though we are blind
we hear this:

Steady trundle of the train under storm clouds
loaded down with malediction,
the radio tower's Babel-bleat to heaven
with the black stone, with the dead for burning
song of electric light, and sleeplessness.

Weariest river at the end of all things
we follow you into the earth.

Ike Whitt

Above the trainyards, in a dying town's wildness
spray-painted over a bible verse, your epitaph
"Ike Whitt lives." You do not.
The painted rock juts above the trees,
the lizards sun themselves.
beer cans and dope bags, dead lighters.
a single, stunted tree climbs from the rocks.

We have never met, you and I
but I recall your death, how
when they pumped your stomach
they found Dilaudid and Aspirin,
birth control pills and vitamins
how you wandered through your party
with your zip lock bag, a pillowcase of pills.
You became an adolescent legend,
our own Keith Moon.

There is no novelty in this. The kids who crush
pills on the stone that bears your name
have never heard of you
and the hills have healed over our footprints
yours and mine. The trainyards rust.
Rats on the river bottom.

The bar stars dim in the daylight,
single file, to graves, a procession.
Too many to spray their names on the rocks.
Too many to remember.

Neva

The closet held everything you left,
your whore's bounty, your abandoned hoard
chinchilla and rabbit skin coats
Black heels my sisters stomped the hall in.
A white cocktail dress, a stack of gossip papers
a book of matches with a dancing girl.
A gold purse filled with swizzle sticks, markers for tricks.
The knife edges of too-small skates. My father's gun.

The pink hallway crumbled
from cheap Moorish arches onto threadbare carpet.
It smelled like the dog, like raw sewage
The hallway blocked by an antique sewing machine.
Boxes of papers and naked newborn mice.
Radio tubes, oxyacetylene welding tanks and rotten pumpkins.
The scrap of other's discarded lives, built into walls.

So no one else could walk out of the same door,
the porch was torn from the house.
The step down to the cinder block, loose in the mud
double my sister's fat legs. How she cried for you.

The middle bedroom with only a mockery of a window
opening into a dirt-floored room filled
with truck tires, with hot water heaters.
old papers, dust, horseflies, ruin.

In the front lawn, a scrawny pine
wore Christmas lights and tinsel in the summertime.
The hedges grown up over the windows
hiding the bare mattress, the hole to the crawlspace
bare pipes and black mud.
My father with dirt under his nails, his infant brothel.
I carry your lie in my mouth even now.
Complicit between you
this stone in my mouth.

With the hope of a new bride
you must have hung the white lace curtains yourself.
Flyspecked and yellow, we held them back,
looking to see when you would return.
We pretended they could cover
what no one thought to see.

The phone on the wall that kept its silence.
The mailbox canted over the swollen ditch,
its mouth open, empty.

In the City of My Birth

In a municipal courthouse, a cutting of a houseplant
stretches white roots into a drinking glass of murky water.
Below those blind roots in a yellowed cabinet
between manila sheets
sits the paper that certifies
that I was born alive, acknowledged by my parents.

Somewhere in the same building are the records of my arrests
for public intoxication.
Nights spent in the blue room
with stars cut out of the plywood, singing.
Marriage certificates of old friends
curl together in that dark.

I have been the awful son of this place
to flee its crumbling buildings and boarded storefronts.
I have left you to die on a dinner plate.

The house of my childhood
with its industrial carpeting
and HUD-approved metal handrails
still squats in its narrow allotment of mud.
A headstone over an empty plot.

Nolda Risener

You owl-white ghost, rheumy, yellow-eyed
your voice a death-beetle tick, a moth wing
deaf as headstones. A tortoise, ancient as god and death
your hands stained paper, nails ivory and cruel.
You terrified.

Great grandchildren dared each other
to tell you a joke, and you'd lean in, slow and terrible
toothless, clouded, not quite blind. Stinking of piss and death.

Old Regular Baptist,
at your graveside no devil's instruments
but a palsied, liver-spotted choir,
in lined-out hymnody sang.

They demanded to open your casket
at the graveside, the grandchildren
that you mothered, and we, their
toy children, too young to be discarded
watched in polyester suits
squinting in Kentucky sun
as they clawed at you.

In your baby-blue casket,
Your dress white as christening.
Your mouth open to sing.

Charles Broughton

The town swallowed your death
in a gas station bathroom.
In the 4am stillness, there is a light
and the coffee pots are filled,
endless vigil of insomniacs,
cigarettes for the sorrowful,
the passing through.

Your road still winds down to the river
the muddy cornstalks, the train trestle.
Young boys still drink there, in the shadow
of the bridge, the catfish jumping.
still crush pills on the toilet tank.

Your house, a rotten tooth in a broken mouth
the bottles piled up in the trash.
Life continues without ceremony
The dead stare through a filmy mirror,
The flickering fluorescent sun.

The Mine Is a Black Mouth

She has fed all her boys to it.
In the hollow of the hills
the mine is an upside down church.
Her boys come back with a blue-black mark no water can erase.
Her boys come back in boxes in their Sunday clothes
then gone back down again.

The mine is family reunion.
The bloodline pools below the earth in the cold and dark.
Her green eyed devil come up every Sunday, to spit, to sing
and fill her belly full of children.

'Till he went down to stay
to wait on Jesus
coming in the middle of the air.

Church of God
With signs following.

The coal cars crawl like rattlesnakes through the topless hills.
Don't it say, *You shall take up serpents?*

They will burn his bones to light the city at night.
She will sit on her porch in the dark
waiting on her devil who will not come.

When the Neighbors Burned a Cross in Our Yard

It was for practice.
They'd never done it before.
They wanted to get it right.
It was not much taller than a first grader, covered in gas and burlap.
They sat around it in lawn chairs, drinking beer. I was ashamed.

Most of our acre hidden from the road
by our house's dirt floor and tarpaper.
A good place for secrets.
They asked permission of my father
It'll be fine, he said, *One more thing not to tell at school.*
Kids raising hell. Just practicing.

A week later, a cross burned in the front yard
of the adopted girl from six houses down
who shared my bus stop.
There were no lawn chairs.

Mary Rita Rakovan

Your bird-brittle bones weighed less
than the casket of my sister's child.
You, dry as down, as cottonwood seeds
the long years cloud the glass.

Your well-scrubbed floor under a sheen of motor oil now
they grind dirt into your carpets
Your clothes, and his hang in the closet
side by side in the room of your death.

There are deer in your garden,
come from along the power lines
to eat the spring shoots.
The Japanese beetles devour your Zinnias.

In the grave, all your forgotten Slovak returns.
The language of a mother country you have never seen.
You whisper back and forth, with Andy
through the entangling roots. Cleveland dissolves.

The war is far away, and you are together
The Wonder Wheel spins above the boardwalk.
The gypsy again, in roller-skates.
You see only this, the soldiers in their uniforms
the girls with stocking seams painted up their legs.

Not your son, his dirty nails, his swallowed mouthful of truths.
Not the host passed over by your family, dutiful in borrowed suits.
Not the blue plastic Madonna with broken hands,
the sardine cans in the sink.

Kindermärchen

One careless word from the father, that bristling bear
and the boys are all turned into blackbirds.
The daughter given in marriage to
the monster that saved you in the woods.
The baby bartered to godfather death.

If your mother buries your bones in the backyard
you will come and sing, and drop a grinding stone around her neck.
If I lose you in the woods you will breadcrumb
home with blood on your hands.
If you meet with a poison apple or a spindle
or lose your shoes, or fall asleep
or dance with dead boys till your clothes are rags
or any one of a million misfortunes
someone will come and kiss your body back from blue sleep.

Parents dance at weddings in iron shoes
roll down hills in barrels full of nails
their bellies stitched shut full of stones
those wolves and grandmothers and giants.

Happy kings lose their daughters to wandering boys
with pockets filled with beans and flutes
with talking cats and singing swords
and all manner of unlikely gimcrackery.

Every task and test and riddle I'd set
even scratching out his eyes, setting him wandering in the desert
even locking him in the tower with the dead men
even sending him to hell itself to sell his salt

cheated with fairies and the devil's mother and
whatever it takes, to steal the child away
to the hollow hill, to the hidden lake
to the other side of the mountain of glass.

Swans and crows and goose-feathered brothers
the dutiful daughter, the dimwitted son, the tailor
all fly over the hills and far away
eventually.

Anthropopathy

I.
In the kitchen, the school of plates
is at last gathered in the shoals of the cabinets.
The oven breathes hot on her neck.
She feeds it a songless bird.
The teapot shrieks, a peacock.
Her hands lift the angry thing
headless and spouting into the cup.
An open mouth that hunger cannot feed.

The television flings shit all over
the vacuumed carpets and clean scrubbed walls
until she throttles it with a switch.
Stands in the silence
barefoot on the carpet's hairy back.

II.
The babies' metal keys have stopped spinning
Does she know?
How my eyes lick her neck.
How I breathe her milk-dreams like a cat
her hair a nest of nightmares.
In the dark, the bed sighs and moans.
The pillows slip from their cases
like the heads of hostages.
While she sleeps, the moon and I stare at each other.

The First Time I Tasted Your Milk

We had between us no children.
You said to me, I *still have a little, always.*
Squeezed your breast in your hand
till it beaded on your sweet brown nipple.
I tasted the tiniest drop of your mercy
that tasted of your skin and your scent
and the way a kiss tastes.
I did not know then you would teach me
to drink it mixed with blood.
Did not know the babies' coming.
Did not know you would become this scaffold of bones
that holds my head aright.

The Northern Country

The robins are starving in the thin snow.
Their blood splashed chests a false fire
in the glass trees.

There is a river that is falling over stone and ice
that has been falling
since the stones ground flour
that now decorate unused parks
an empty museum, with a gift shop.

Each day, I sit in a half-burned down factory
where thirty-six men burned to death
beetled on the edge of the cliff.

From the empty office across the hall
the water is steady as time
the water that carried a trained bear over the falls
that killed Sam Patch the daredevil, in 1829.

The engines that ran the streetcars
rust in a disused bar's basement
and the river, indifferent to living and dead
drops through the broken wheelhouse
riming the bones of abandoned scaffolding with ice.

This brutal country
still half wild beneath suburban streets.
Hotels and whorehouses safely shuttered.

At night, with my hound howling
at the swollen udders of the moon
trying to hang himself with his leash
we chase deer across the frozen lawns.

Leviathan

You are an eyeless totem, a bagged cadaver papoose.
A broken bottle, engineblack and gasoline in water.
Here is your house, fish in the leafless trees.
Catfish, barbed, electric and swollen in tall grass that sways.
Invisible mover you do not speak.

The dead gather in your devil's chapel, under the steel-grey water.
How you shook like a puppet the last time I saw you,
pale as a hospital. There are sturgeon, fished for with the hooks
of cranes. Their bellies filled with glistening black eggs, salt fruit.

Here are the swollen ditches in the spring.
Frogs with pale appendages dangling, useless and poisoned.
Here is foxfire and lantern light.
Here is a hand in the dark.
Cloudy ice blocks the sun, the muddy hole.
Here is your black book of engines I never learned.
Here the fire that ate your rotted curtains.
Here the broken shells, the fossils in the limestone driveway.
Sea bed bones broken into gravel road.
Black tar liquid in the heat.

Here the cars rusted on their axles dissolving in the mud.
Here the eyes of mice in the farmhouse.
Here is a sea-bottom of wheat.
A ghost of a pig, a chickenhouse smell.
A flooded field of rotten cornstalks.

Flying Dutchman, Saint's fire, Jonah
Your fury comes behind you with its chrome teeth
to swallow you down to hell.
You spoon.
You feather.
You rust hooked worm.
The fungus gathers on the oak of you.

Lightning struck and hollow, ripe and rotten for the fire.
Sick with prophecy, a scarecrow stuffed with doom.
Cuyahoga oilslick, poison water.
A cracked bell ringing in the drowned town.

Pica

First, she swallowed her words.
They whispered in her belly's kitchen and the hallways of veins.
She ate her fingernails sharp, to points.
She ate a crucifix on a chain like an anchor.
She swallowed her tongue, and air.
She ate a rope of hair, to climb out, but still he came.
So she ate a box of nails and a hammer, and a pinewood plank.
She built a house to live in.
He crawled inside her like a tapeworm
and lived in her drainpipes in a clot of unsaid things.
So she ate a box of candles and a book of matches.
He blew them out and came in the dark.
She ate a string of light bulbs just to be safe.
She opened her mouth, and it was dark still.
So she ate the streetlight, and the sun.
Ate the stars and the planets.
Ate airplanes and jack-o-lanterns until
there was only the black and he was the black.
She ate that too.
Switchblade motor oil thick and greasy.
Brittle as a mirror back, tar sticky.
Broken combs and crow feathers.
Iron and tires and asphalt and highway at night.
Until there was nothing left.
Then she ate the nothing.

Eric Deer

Red-faced, unfinished, hand curved to hold the hammer.
A life scratched on notebook paper
I remember you, clean.
Reading and building in a store filled with old paperbacks
not comatose on that lawyer's floor,
veins full of Fentanyl, as they lied over you
your time already finished
Your father, sharer of needles,
fled the scene.

There was a wave behind you,
of dead boys and shrinking funerals
the festival gone out of it.
After a while only the family shows up.

Death was still novel then.
and hung over in a five dollar suit
the soles of my shoes cracking
I went in and spoke to you.

You held your daughter's picture in your hand.
The flowers and doilies
of that room were suffocating
as your mother gawked at your exotic friends
and after, we drank and did not sing.

We asked your family for your notebooks
the illegible poems and stories,
but they did not understand.
We wanted to hold some piece of you
as you spilled into the ground, and the quiet fell
so they gave us nothing.

I found some loose pages, after
in a borrowed book, unfinished drafts
unreadable now, a crooked scrawl against the lines.

Sam Patch

"Some things can be done as well as others."—Sam Patch

The gulls cry at the base of the falls,
a ravenous and expectant mob
they are clean and white
like cotton in the mill,
the child's hand spanning it
a host of angels.

You, drunk, with a trained bear,
a fox on a chain, jumping from the mill, from the masts
of moored ships, from a rickety platform
on goat island. You strike-instigator. You spectacle.
You stone against god's window, fever-tinged
How the proper ladies gathered,
the gentle folks tittilated to see you
romance your death, dance with it.

How you fell, headlong the last time
they believing you were hidden in the cave
watching and laughing, finishing your bottle.
The preachers railed against their sheep,
for their need for a wonder.

They could not accept their own muddy hands
all those clean white gulls, their open mouthed awe
and hunger, and you, wingless, uplifted in the spray
dead beneath the ice, buried with a wooden placard.

The Lady and the Tiger

She imagined rain or fog
something cinematic, soft focus.
The night is clear when it comes.

She hops the cast iron fence
runs through pebbled paths to their assignation.
His roar rings through the park.
In the dark, drowsy watchmen
sneaking cigarettes, ignore her.

She knows without her he would starve;
cartoon-pink steaks cut from sickly antelope
could never sustain him.

He was born to this, no memory of India.
His paws remain sheathed in velvet pads.
His piebald coat and broken teeth pain him.

She knows he will not fail her
he has obligingly leapt through fire
for those who loved him less.

He paces the pattern of his cage
free of the tedium of circuses.
She wants to give him a sort of proof
some small and private justice.
A pile of clothes to puzzle the zookeepers.
She is new, and naked.

She climbs into his enclosure of false stone
and like a lamb gives herself over
to the ruin of his mouth.

Disappearing Trick

When you are curved into yourself
a Moebius strip wrapped around
the missing-tooth ache of your heart
I am a fat drunk horsefly
clumsy legs skittering over
the smooth surface of your inside-out skin
the backs of your eyes.

You are gone. A little girl pulled down the drain
with the bathwater, the ducks and boats, the soap
and sun and stars drawn down the spiral
of water into the ringing pipes.

I am that ring of shaving scum
that never goes down.
Something small and venomous
climbing out of the drain.

When Wishing Still Helped

There was a girl who unmade her mother.
Spat back her borrowed milk
unhitched her bones from the mud.

Her father thought to lash her to the earth
but she was already rising.
His belt could no more
hold her than you could hold the moon
from turning away her face.

She made herself a skin of stories,
stretched the names of her friends over her good strong arms
from the sky she took the oldest stars.
Set them spinning in the mouths of children.

In her wrath she could spit lightning
that would crack stones like ice.
In her sorrow came a host of winters.
Wolves that hungered for the sun.

Her laughter is music, is music for always
and this could never be one of her songs.

Cybele Agdistis

Without invocation. No summoning rattle of barbarous tongues,
No sigil to scratch around circles and mirrors.
In the clock of heaven, this gear is nameless,
this broken tooth in the mouth, this un-dreaming.
Silence of half an hour, eye of the maelstrom,
intake of breath before trumpets.
There is no prophecy here, the cards all pasteboard blanks
blank river stones drawn from a bag one after another,
the tea refusing shape, a lineless palm, an empty newspaper.

Here is a mute and eyeless idol
Here a headless god, a broken clay hand
a cloth poppet that has lost it's buttons.
A nameless, swordless angel, a forgotten word.

Before You Were Born

Your small gallop ran circles in your mother.
I had not known love could eat the world.
Your two hearts so small, thundering
the world so brittle-bright.

A drowned man sang with a broken voice.
You came, in a blue panic
a knotted rope around your neck.
Your aunt held your mother's hand
I stood, overwhelmed with joy and terror and
a kicked hornet's nest of doctors.

Under lights, at first she could not hold you
so I told you to her, like a story.
Your hands strong, the wet pooled still
in your eyes, each song of your breath
until they consented to give you
to that world that you left,
the sweet home and hive that is your mother.

From you I learned to demand sweetness for her.
Learned the terror of your loss before your first breath.
Learned how she has broken herself again and again
to bring such wonders to the world.

You six, who are one, who are my heart
have taught me what it is to be a man.
What a life is, what price hangs from it.
How quickly I would lay mine down
for one more breath of yours.

On the Old Bright Sea the Moon Keeps Grinning in

God's boat blew her seals
and threw black smoke
and all the oil monkeys went over the side
and he threw down a hook
in the Devil's green mouth
and that scaly bastard dragged them to shore
and the walls of the city were jasper and gold
and God lost his pay in a game of dice
and got drunk and in a fight
and woke up in jail with a headache
and a pocketful of dancehall tickets
and a press gang took him
and threw him on a gunship
and the sun was a plum

and the bullets sang *death death death*

and a boy come falling out of the sky with his wings on fire
and right in God's lap
and God's girl got a purple heart in a box
and a widow's pension
and the moon just kept on grinning.

In the Menagerie, in the Mud

We are greeted by rhinoceros
tapping horns over a mouthful of hay.
A branchless tree filled with tires and windchimes
a punching bag. Little birds hop
in the stagnant water that fills their footprints.

The children mill around your feet
our boy peering out through a shark's mouth
our girl teetering atop this newly borrowed body.

They face each other like rail cars
in collision, stormclouds
sumo wrestlers in the mud.

Leather behemoths, creaking, the delicate hair of their ears
pennants in the slightest breeze
the long hard slope of their foreheads
bony as triceratops.

You, and I, and our half-healed scars walk together.
The little birds sing at our feet.

Motherless

You had no home to hold you.

Your cardboard box open to the sky
behind the garage, among the rusting sheet metal.
The willow wept.

The rabbits lived until the snow came,
starved in their crates unfed by we lazy children
but you would not survive the day.

My sisters did not think to pray.
Their white dresses and bonnets for show
a masque of piety, my father refusing the host
and bloody Christ staring at the ceiling
through the endless morning.

We ate what sweetness we could find.
My dog, loose from the flagpole,
prowling the grass
for another small and unwatched thing.

In the Rafters Our Son Has Built a Nest

of all the un-taken out garbage, wet black plastic
milk bottles full of borrowed anger.
He is trying it on, a wig, a dead soldier's uniform in an attic trunk
a cloudy salute in the mirror.

When I sleep, it is cave-black, memoryless.
I wake with my hands full
a broken piece of diving mask in my hands
a mouth full of library paste and missing teeth
the stripes you laid across my back.

There's a worm in me, a black fly rattle.
When we were young, I burned my garbage
I cannot unremember the smell, the blue-green flame
how we watched the pages turn back, naked women writhe
in oil and potato peelings, toothy smiles curling
in the midden heaps of secrets, of broken dishes
how the black eyes of the mice
stared out of every corner, the paperwasp walls
black grease and the devil's radio.

All the chickens clustered in the rain, the door to ruin.
Every house has a secret room you find in dreams
where the unsaid things and the dust
and the king of the mice, and the unforgotten insults sleep
a still filled with rotten mash
a library of coverless books.

Even the stars curve inward on themselves and go black
chasing their own hearts down a stairwell
where no light can escape, and the detritus of worlds
spins and collides in the hollow dark.

From the first fire, we are fleeing and falling
to ruin and cold, time itself a wound spring

in a junkheap alarm clock, radium dials glowing
for the sowbugs and silverfish
a stateroom on a sunken oceanliner
and heat-death inevitable as sundown
still I wake with you.
Take out the trash on the way to work.

Ted O'Neil

In the windowless Union Bar and Grill
the painted goat quoted Heidegger
"Existence is in the form of a question"
and we, dumb and young and full of Schlitz
gathered around the burned boat you left behind you
and were starless.

The day the haterock died,
I hated God and Texas
Both left you on the floor.
Your brain was dead
and your body followed.

Yesterday, on the radio
I heard a song from nineteen years ago.
It was not yours.

There is a procession,
with pinhole cameras in their bones,
with men in bottles, a patent medicine tent revival
a smalltown parade of car crash and almost.
You go into the dimming light as we forget
forget the body's abandon and roar of blood and breath.

The ghosts gather thick around the bar, remembered smoke
moths hurling themselves against the incandescent,
the spirit yellow in glass.
The townies sway a nineteen-year-old kid
beats the shit out of a pawnshop drumkit.

The Women With the Heads of Birds

are singing in the bright place.
Their tongues stitch bright bones with flowers.
On the final beach, atomic eggs on white sand.
The vanishing point a well of ending.
The pail drops down, the water ringing in the dark dark dark.
The women spit stars in the wormy eyes of sailors.
O my soul, have mercy.
When I am stripped beyond naked.
When I am undone, a mouthful of ash.
When I am come at last to the hollow city's drowned battlements.
When I have stretched my skin's boat across these splintered ribs
and sailed beyond the edges of the world.
O my kindly one, have mercy.

Boatmen stand in the bright blast of heaven,
scraps of film develop in their pockets, tattered insignia
dropping among the bone thickets, the copper briars.
Still you spin out the promise of thrones, powers, dominions.

Flowers turn their deaf heads towards the sun.
In the windless calm, among the blooms,
sirens sing a mantic song.
Prophesy to the worms. Because the end of beauty is death.

When I am come at last to that shore I will carry your name
in my mouth, a bird with the head of a woman.
Your fingers hooked in my collarbones.
Your breath in the windy hollow of my skull.

In the marsh.
In the islands in the sea of milk.
The labyrinths of my days unwound
and you, spinner of my days
perch at the end of all threads and ways
at the end of all tales.

O my bird.
O my tongue's confusion.
O heaven, be with me even past the end.
Where the cold rocks scrape their tracks around the sun
Where the radio coughs out its last, in the icelight of stars.

The Air Is Thick as a Tongue

The piano has pumpkins in its teeth
rivers of cats in bags, broken brick foundations
catfish and weeds.
The piano is asleep, dreaming
of parking lot gulls, of trashheaps and bonfires
and the teeth of elephants, of iron nails
it's a logjam in a river, and the silence piles up.

The birdcage has a doll in it
and maybe that's enough, maybe it never liked
the wild bird it held inside it.
The shining black eye of its terror.
We apes, poking seed through the bars.

The bird is dead.
It's snowing into the tulips.
The mice have left your attic.
Your vigil and your silence still squat upstairs
and comb their long and greasy hair.

We played your records.
The piano was dreaming of the harp in its stomach.
The records said the same thing they always do
and stopped when they came to the end, again.

Hyracotherium

At first my sister's horse
was only a handspan, pocket size.
Almost a toy, except for the way it ran circles on the tabletop
knocking over the gravy boat
drinking from upturned water glasses
leaving hoof prints in the butter.

My mother said, *pay it no mind.*
It grazed on my salad and shit in the mashed potatoes.
Slowly, at first, then quickly it grew.
A struggling puppy, it bit our hands.
Tongued the sugar bowl.
My sister drank.
The horse ran around the table
snorting and soaked with frenzy.
She chewed.

Is the beef too tough? I asked.
The horse ran up the stairs, knocking family photographs off the wall.
My wife passed bread and salt around the table, but my sister
did not take any, as her horse
now fifteen hands high
nickered and ran up the attic steps
eyes rolling, hooves drumming the wooden floor
so we could no longer pretend to speak.

Written on the Occasion of Terry Thompson's Suicide, Zanesville, OH

I am of this place,
and when I release my bestiary
it will be a king of rats that crawls from my gut,
a tangle of tales and black eyes
a cloud of blowflies,
to sing in the eaves of my final room
a possum hissing wrath, a black bear

save this sad, mute ape, who will shed my skin
at the last like a salvation army suit
and carry your name into the canopy of the trees.

You grieved the nineteen tigers, the lion chasing horses
the wolf, the storm of animals
and how I love you for that
to love the sharp teeth let loose in the mown lawns
the hungry bear in the pantry
to hate the safety of bullets
the black stain of a beastless road
to love the wolf, and hate the keeper's skin.

Mary Celeste

A ghost ship hung with yellow lamps
foundered on the reef of the morning.
My little school huddles in their private sleep
the shadows of their terrors
passing over and away.

The bed you left
the plate and the bones, such
rags as have draped around you
but you are gone.

Here the mast I have lashed myself to
the jackline of your hands untied.
Here Scylla. Here poppies.
Here your song still hangs
above the wave and seabird
and the starless dark.
Here shipworm heart in the carved and painted girl.

Birds throng the crosstrees.
It is good Friday.
The sun and the moon-pulled water rise
and you are coming home.

Arcadia

You queen of the flowering dark come crawling
from mud, a supplication of satellites.
Lily in the graveyard, flight of doves.
You are the skin's book
the dance of farmwives on the mountain.

I am black gravepit.
Bonepile and ash, knife edge
black goat and cockerel, blood in the furrow.
I am terror, and slaughter of lambs
The winter's teeth.

Build fires of old doors, unloved books
Unsent letters, linen closet of ghosts.
Let her come pale out of dark.
Her bones, her flowers, green tendrils twist from cold mud.
Flowering bulbs, swollen and strange, a wolf's purse.

A man, standing on a mountaintop in the right light
throws his shadow on the clouds, a Colossus.

Crown him, wrap him in hides
Still I know him, let them dance back to back
In the dark, still I know them
Bring your book, devil, your stained turnips, your black wine

Turn the world over and burn it down
the rotted scraps of history in an atomic singularity,
a bonfire of yesterdays.

Still I know you, cold May morning sun
Lonely shepherd, scarecrow on a stick
Crown of black-winged birds.

Here is a dish of milk in the hedgerow.
Here is a twist of salt in your pocket.
Here is iron and bright silver.
a rhyme against the dark
a prayer for spring.

Honey in the Lion's Head

When Jay Wright found the shark's jawbone
he was seven hundred feet below the ground
in the mine's dark ocean.
It was black on black, polished as coal
a rictus of three hundred million years wait for
a hillbilly hand to free it from the stone.
Only the teeth remain
as though time swallows all malice, all thought
all hearts and bones and terrors
leaving only hunger, only want
only teeth to wait, scissor-sharp
in the secret and dark places four miles down.
They dragged it into the light
marveled at the size of it.
The doorway-mouth of that black place.

A Hidden Constellation

in the banknotes keeps them safe from photocopiers
the peasants dream of wealth, that neverending horn
saltgrinder in the bottom of the sea
tablecloth of the devil's sooty brother
your suite at the plaza, your Paris apartment.

We burn our bills in the fireplace
blue flame of the hours, of blood, ash tally marks on a slate of days
a sweet for the baby, a dress, a house, measured hours.
My life, wrapped in a bouquet of bills
an idol of clock arms and cutoff dates
an endless succession of numbers and spreadsheets
of recipes and things to be nailed, one to the other.

On an altar, surrounded by the perfume of the archangel
by the glittering skull, by the saints and rabbits
is the hour of the morning
when you are mine alone.
When I am in the house we carry between us
like a tortoise shell on the back of an elephant
the littlest ones asleep, unknowing.
When we are only who and what we are.
The dead world breathes.
The smallest leaves pull their shoulders up through the dirt.

In this hour is paradise, in this hour are all scales balanced.
We burn ghost money engraved with the Jade Emperor, The Bank of Hell
burn paper-mache Rolls Royces and televisions repaying debts
give coins to the boatman, flowers for the dead, fruit for the god.

Here is this unsteady light we have shored between us:
against the hungry, the empty, the lonely
squatting at the end of the streetlights
shored against the crocodile teeth of the sky.
Our sleeping boy's head, filled with sugar sharks

with fish in cages, these porcelain lambs, these rabbits
this sweetness in the face of the dark.

Familiar as a Suit of Second-Hand Clothes

Sorrow scratches at the door to be let in.
A cast off skin, your tongue rolls round the words it says
like something eaten in the dark.
A three piece suit sits up, walks over
sits down in your chair—
It *looks like it still fits,*
you think.
But you are fading already, another bad idea.
The new shape stands,
walks across the house.
Washes a face in the bathroom sink.
Stares back as you shave.

Cold water and soap filming over, never rinsing clean.

It is fine without you.
It knows the tricks you taught it.
How to slow your breath and fall into sleep.
How to chew and swallow, smile and speak.

You might as well curl up inside it.
Lean your head against your belly's skin, a cold car window.
Let it drive.
The moon will hold even with you.
The stars unchanging.
The miles will pass unseen, unmissed.

Of the Coming of the Companions of God to Eire

In 673 there was a comet, and a star of great brightness
Seen in the months of September and October.
In the year of our lord 690 it rained blood in Leinster.
Butter in the churn turned to flesh and blood.
A wolf spoke with a human voice.
The sea between Ireland and Scotland froze solid
And there was travel across the ice.

In the year of our lord 721 in the monastery of Clonmacnoise
While the monks were at prayer a ship was seen,
her sails filled with wind sailing above the round tower,
In the upper air, where the fallen angels throng thick as fish
and a great iron anchor was heav'd over her side
and dragged in the dust of the street
and into the church, till it stuck fast under the altar.

The chronicle tells us that the monks were sore afraid
when a sailor swam down the rope
to pull it free, and they saw him drowning
in the goodly air, and rushed then to his aid
to pull the anchor free, and the ship sailed on
with no word of human language shared.

In 734 there was the appearance of a dragon
"both huge and ugly to behold
And a great thunder heard after him in the firmament."
In 743 an awful marvelous sign was seen in the stars.
In 745 in the night a terrible and wondrous sign appeared
amongst the stars.

in 759 three showers fell in Crich-Muireadhaigh in Inishowen.
First pure silver of an unknown working
Then a shower of wheat, and last a shower of honey
Of a fair and rich flavour.
In 760 fire came from Heaven and slew men in Dearthach Aedhain

In 765 "a terrible and wonderful prodigy
appeared among the stars."

In 805, the Ceile De, the clients and companions of god
came over the sea with dry feet, without a vessel
and a scroll was given them to preach
out of heaven and carried up again when the sermon
was finished.

This year, cakes and bread bled when cut
and the birds spoke with human voices.

Evidence

I will give back the armless engineer I put in my pocket
his moustaches curling in the dark, over my lips, thick as secrets.
The songless egg I put my thumb through.
The naked heads of the mice before they went under
when I drowned them all with a wooden spoon.
The cat I left in the tall grass, the ruined house.

I will return the bloody girl by the carnival stone.
The envelope of money behind the bar.
The purse left behind in a phone booth.

I will relinquish every broken window, every brick
every dumpster fire, kicked mailbox, candy bar, book
the forty-two trumps, every breath.
Blood daisies, gravestone roses, concrete saints
the furniture of churches, all returned.
How many pounds of salt?
How many hours of your good heart pumping?
Your voice on a wire this book of lead, these millstone promises
this broken lock.

I should have snipped off my hands.
Filled my lungs with coal
should have stitched a barrel of nails in my belly
and drank from cold deep water.
Should have fallen down the chimney into the cooking pot.

I want a vinegar-scrubbed plate of a heart.
White linen on a laundry cart
my angel-collar boiled in starch.
I want warm snow, cold fire, crumbless time
with hospital corners, bleached history,
and a forever of clocks to give to you.

She Opened Her Mouth

The river came out, whiskey and catfish, fog and brown water.
A barrel-house woman sang knives and razors and done-me-wrong.
She carried her like a secret everybody knows
'till she could wail, bright eyed
'till the music fell back and went away
'till the angels pulled their turkey-buzzard wings over their eyes
'till the clocks hung their mouths open.
A long sweet lonesome note that crawled into your guts.

Singing: *blood river, heart, sun behind fog*
the bone hills, the morning, rock and antler
Song tearing you down and stitching you, rag and quilt.
A name you had forgotten.
A hymn in a graveyard of teeth.
Hillbilly praise, crooked as a coal vein.

You always knew, plain and homespun
simple as morning, Jesus knocking on the door
of her throat, *whiskey river coal barge*
simple as truth, birds against the sun.
A gun in a hall closet.
Deer in the corn.

A Flaming Sword, Also

When she died, he began gardening
none of the neighbors close enough
to see the penciled labels.
Wolfpeach for tomatoes.
Gall, bitterroot, rampion, insurance fire
Her lips, strawberries
last Thursday, blackberry bramble
the grass meticulously cut, the walkway swept.

Every day, he walked Memory.
Who pulled the leash and fought.
Who pissed the grass and burned it yellow.
He carried home a stone.
They piled around the garden in a loose wall.
The pips from her last apple grew in the center.
A riot of birds the color of her hair
laughed in the branches.

The neighbors did not think of him at all
until they found him, in the evening.
Still holding the bloody saw.
The rib on the blanket labeled in his careful hand.

Dick Clark

It is New Years Eve in the city of the dead
and they are playing all your favorite records
the 45s your sisters broke, your grandfather's box
of 78s that burned with the house.
The tape unspooled in your first car.

When the ball drops, it is the sun itself
going down into the wintry dark.
The dead stand crowded in the street
The cold blows ticker tape through them

He is the oldest teenager,
His teeth reflect the borrowed light
like the moon's sliver
and the kids twist

He plays the unsaid apologies,
plays all the thrown away declarations of love
the burned letters, the swallowed words.
He is officiate of this rite,
and without him, the world has lost a priest
for the living, the years have stopped
rock and roll, contrary to expectation, has died.
in the city of the dead, they stay up late.

Let's twist again, like we did last summer

and you taste it in your mouth
cicadas and lemon, wild Irish rose
crackle of the radio.

Rich Weiss

We rode the freight trains into town
jumping off when they picked up speed
and sliding down the rock embankments.
A sign on a post, covered in rust, bullet holes
advertised a long-closed window and siding company
Exteriors Of Time, fields of corn and wheat,
a go-kart track, the weird sculptures of Mini Golf
under fluorescent lights, a dingy arcade where metal bands
played in the parking lot, a whirling pit over the gravel.

Rich was older, had better weed,
drank stolen airplane bottles of "cocktail" and "martini"
with us, hopped cemetery fences, showed us how to make a pipe
from tin foil and a pen, from soda cans and apples.
Rich, on Dilaudid, or Codeine, or Valium and Whiskey,
alone, a drunk, stumbling scarecrow
(or asleep on the tracks, depending on who was telling)
was hit by the Burlington Northern,
and his heart stopped.

The paramedics jump-started him,
and Rich came back, Electric Lazarus
with cinematic tales of a white light, of voices
of being spat back into the world,
which he would tell while we huffed gas,
drank Everclear, shook with stolen speed.

I do not recall the method of his second death.

Jenny Greenteeth

squats in mud and duckweed
with her broken mouth.
She is a swallower of apple-cheeked babies
riverwitch, the willow's lover
sweetheart of suicides.

Jenny Greenteeth has weedy hair
and long bony fingers, to clutch at the ankles
of boys skipping stones, swinging from ropes.
She is the tangler of fishing lines.
Her teeth are broken bottles.

Jenny Greenteeth combs her hair
and children piss their beds.
She is the dark, and the man in the windowless car.
She will take what is left when he is done.

Jenny is the fish that eat the eyes of the broken dollies.
She hisses in the grass at the water's edge.
Jenny is the lover of the boy with the pocketfuls of stones.
Jenny fills her bed with cold water on the nights he comes.
She is swallower of crime and sorrow.

She is the branches where the drowned boy tangled.
The rot that puffed his belly in the cold and the dark.
The kiss that took his lips when he rocked in her arms for a fortnight.

Riverwitch, hungry lover, her splintered mouth whispers
how they knew her once.
She could teach a secret song
to charm the fish, to knot the wind
to swell the bellies of the kine.

How the river rose, black with mud
for the crop before they broke her.

How they gave her bones and blood for barley
for their beer, called her mother
for the good black earth
she left behind her.
Now she is hungry, and the weed
a green carpet of scum, runoff rich
tastes of oil and poison.
Jenny remembers songs to reap to,
remembers lovers in her good black mud
fires in the autumn, remembers dollies of corn.

She waits and whispers in the dark and mud
for the babies with their apple cheeks
for night swimmers, for the sorrow-laden
to come down the weedy shadow
to riverwitch, and unfed dark.

Jehan de Mandeville, Returned From the East, Orders His Affairs

On Michaelmas day, when the divil fell from heaven, we took to the sea and it was a black going and long ways we came at last to the holy land, under letters from the Sultan, I saw the blood stained rock where our lord Jesus died and going further then we came to the sea of Ind where adamant stones bristle with the masts of ships and iron, and going on, went through that valley where the head of the divil stands, and saw the heaps of gold and murdered men and touched them not, and came round at last to the kingdom of Prester John.

And what telling is there of that black king, and the wonders and terrors of his land?

How they honored their dead, throwing gobbets of flesh to the vultures and called them angels, come to take them to heaven, and drank toasts to their fathers from the brimming bowl of their skulls and yet marched the cross before them into battle, and how I kissed the yellow robes of the patriarch, of St. Thomas the doubter. In the north of that land there is a wall of steel, set by Alexander, who they call Dulkannon, to bind Gog and Magog, till such time as the earth shall cast it asunder, and beyond that end we could not travel. In Tartary I drank once, from a well they said could keep a man from death, but now, in my own country, swollen with gout and wonders, I await the opening of that other door, that other angel, blacker than vultures against the sun, I await departure for that other kingdom, that other king.

Method of Locii

I think I dreamt you in our bed
milk-soaked, snoring sweetly.
Our house filled, a party with pictures out of magazines.
Our babies baking cakes in a tiny oven
to celebrate the holiday of your apparition.

Streamers hung, balloons like latex lungs filled
with your breath, the ghost that haunts this house
I drew a bath, you rose from the foam
our daughter perched on your shining tail.

We eat our dinner at a polished table
with an empty seat, the ever-invited guest.
The house quiet, and dark.
You fever-bright
burning up the road, again.

Wax Bloom, Willow Beauty

There was a plum tree in our yard
that grew fruit only once,
dark and unspeakably sweet
then never grew them again.

Though the bees crawled through the blossoms,
though the pears fell soft and rotten
and the wasps came to drink their broken sweetness
there were no plums. No November Moth.
The house is gone to ash, to broken plates in dirt
to a driveway and a septic tank and a garage full of parts.
The bicycles rusted into the clay, the fruitless tree twisted.
Years later, a summer, and a broken heart
and in someone's yard, a heavy laden tree,
plums dropping on the sidewalk, ignored.
That infrequent flavor of flowers, of perfume
that gorging on sweetness,
who can say when it will come?

Catherine O'Leary's Cow

leaves the lamp unkicked and bottles three days in October.
The streets of the city never change, there is no second star.
Wooden boardwalks line the lake
a town with smaller shoulders.
The slaughterhouses and criminals lack
a grandeur, the knot of railroads untied.
On a gravel street that divides two counties
the crumbling house I dream is never built.

Unbuild it now—strip siding down to mirror
reflection of insulation, wood framing.
Nails crawl to ore, to slag.
Cement-block foundations dissolve to dust
lumber unburns, planks inchworm and root.

There is no hollow woodgrain door
to stand before, with flashlight in hand.
There is no regret, no Bluebeard refrain in my head
of every door save this one
behind which all my terror and my sorrow flow.
No imagined woodsman's axe to swing
and split his hairy belly throat to crotch
release the clot of ghosts I've stuffed this scarecrow with.

My sisters do not stop here,
wear their ages like borrowed clothes
and I, when we meet, have no wager against your sorrow,
cannot understand
your tattooed tear, your graveyard arms.
Can never match your hunger
or know the way a city is rebuilt from ruin
so we part strangers in a smaller country.

Let time come as it must.
Let Pegleg Sullivan steal the milk.
Let the world end, if it ends in you.

Jacob Rakovan is an Appalachian writer in diaspora. He is a 2011 New York Foundation for the Arts Fellow in Poetry and recipient of a 2013 National Endowment for the Arts Fellowship. His work has appeared in numerous journals including *The Dead Mule School of Southern Literature, The James Dickey Review, Anon, Thrush and Phantom Drift: A Journal of New Fabulism* as well as anthologies by Salmon Poetry Press, MTV Books and The Arsenic Lobster. Rakovan was a finalist for the 2012 Linda Bruckheimer Series in Kentucky Literature and the Gell poetry prize and has been nominated for a Pushcart Prize and Dzanc book's *Best of the Web*. He is co-curator of the Poetry & Pie Night reading series in upstate New York, where he resides with his five children and a mermaid.

Acknowledgements

"The River Is for Drowning Girls" first published in *The Dead Mule School of Southern Literature*
"Kindermärchen," "Ingrid Elizabeth Deardoff," "She Opened Her Mouth," "Disappearing Trick," and "Catherine O'Leary's Cow" first published in *Nailed Magazine*
"Hyracotherium" first published in *Anon*
"Pica" and "The First Time I Tasted Your Milk" first published in *Ocean State Review*
"In the Northern Country" first published in *ghoti*
"In the Menagerie, In the Mud" first published in *Arsenic Lobster*
"Monee, Illinois Can Go to Hell" first published in *The Dead Mule School of Southern Literature*
A version of "A Bedsheet Ghost" first published in *James Dickey Review* as "On the Night You Died"
"The Mine Is a Black Mouth" first published in *The National Endowment For The Arts* (web)
"Anthropopathy" first published in *Cavalier Literary Couture*
"The Women With the Heads of Birds" first published in *The Anemone Sidecar*
"The Air Is Thick as a Tongue" first published in *Thrush*
"Jehan de Mandeville, Returned From the East, Orders His Affairs" first published in *Lacuna*
"(After *Child Ballad #44*)" first published in *Matchbook*
"Arcadia" first published in *Mirror Dance*
"The Lady and the Tiger" first published in *Exterminating Angel*
"Jenny Greenteeth," and "The Man Who Made the Nightingale," first published in *Phantom Drift: A Journal of New Fabulism*
"Leviathan" first published in *Phantom Drift: A Journal of New Fabulism*
"Hilt's Law"first published in *Split This Rock*
"On the Old Bright Sea the Moon Keeps Grinning in," "Wax Bloom, Willow Beauty," and "In the Rafters Our Son Has Built a Nest" first published in *Hanging Loose Magazine*

Thank you to Rachel McKibbens for the never-ending inspiring light of your existence, and for having the strongest radio signal in the world. Thank you Anthone Garcia, Piper Jane Austin, Holden Matthew Vance, Clementine McQueen Rakovan and Lulu Shazzam Remedios Rakovan for your love, support, and for allowing both of your parents to be artists as well as makers-of-grilled-cheese and answerers-of-questions. Thank you to Elizabeth Rakovan, for each day. Thank you to the women of the Pink Door Writing Retreat for your bravery and honesty, for allowing me the rare gift of your company and the opportunity to assist you in the crucial work you do. Thank you to all our Poetry & Pie Night family for keeping poetry and community always at the forefront. Also, for the pie. Thank you to Josh and Karyn Justice. Thank you to Herbert Eugene Roe. Thank you to David Forman, my indefatigable reader, and relentless cheerleader. Thank you Carrie Seitzinger for your editorial eye and for taking a pile of poems and helping me find a book in them. Matty Byloos for your dedication to poetry over all economic sense. Thank you to the people of Portsmouth, Ohio and throughout Appalachia for your continued survival in the face of a culture that would happily eradicate you. Thank you for your song.

SMALL DOGGIES PRESS

Artful Fiction & Poetry
For Lovers of the Written Word

Small Doggies Press supports, defends, and publishes the most beautiful, challenging, and artful prose and poetry that we can find. We believe that the author has all the power, and our job is to create a context within which they, and most importantly their work, can flourish and find the intelligent, curious readership that it deserves.

Small Doggies Press is a division of Small Doggies Omnimedia, LLC, an Oregon Corp.

Other titles available from

SMALL DOGGIES PRESS

Into the Dark & Emptying Field is an interrogation of loneliness and its many masks. It explores innocence as the price of knowledge in a host of voices that share an emotional truth. McKibbens offers a monument of understanding for even the bleakest pieces of our human conundrum.

Into the Dark & Emptying Field

poems by **Rachel McKiddens**

$14.95 | 88 pages | 5.5" × 8.5" | softcover | ISBN: 978-0-9848744-3-9

"Hard and as real as the ax blade, the poems in *Into the Dark & Emptying Field* are unapologetically fierce and undeniably gorgeous. Strikingly imaginative and expertly crafted, these necessary poems shine a dubious flashlight on both the menace and the marvel that surrounds us. Otherworldly and at times shockingly brutal, McKibbens' work is both crucial and addictive."

—**ADA LIMÓN**

"Rachel McKibbens' work shatters me and my world, then pieces us back together on the page like no other poetry I have ever read, creating a new reality, a self that feels what I cannot feel, sees what I cannot see. These poems are at once dreamscapes and yet as solid and real as stones in my hands, stones I want to press against my chest forever, then hurl back into the infinity of space where words of such beauty and power surely come from."

—**RICHARD BLANCO**

"The ancient Japanese swordsmiths categorized a sword by how many body parts it could pass through, i.e., a two-neck sword, a three-arm sword...The strongest and deadliest was a four-torso sword. This book is a four-torso sword. You will feel it, hard."

—**JENNIFER L. KNOX**

Other titles available from

SMALL DOGGIES PRESS

After murdering his elder brother, Marlet must flee the broken town of Victory. With his sword, our low-hung handed hero maneuvers his way through a decrepit southern desert murdering blank-skinned men, being pursued by his illegitimate son, and deceiving those he encounters. All the while, Marlet holds on to his precious memories of Edie, the widowed wife of his brother.

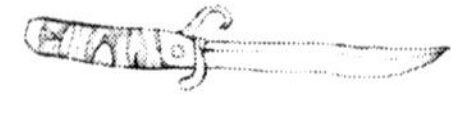

Edie & the Low-Hung Hands

by **Brian Allen Carr**

fiction | $12.95 | 132 pages | 5.5" × 8.5" | softcover | ISBN: 978-0-9848744-2-2

"In turns naturalistic and fantastic, Brian Allen Carr has crafted a truly original tale. This Texas landscape is a mix of country and blues. Larry McMurtry sings Robert Johnson. And then there's the sword."

—Percival Everett, author of *Assumption* and *I Am Not Sidney Poitier*

"This book is beautiful. You're going to hell if you don't buy it. I mean that. Carr is a man with magic inside his heat. Read this book and meet a man who will love you forever. Live. Live. Read Carr. You will be alive. FINALLY."

—Scott McClanahan, author of *Crapalachia* and *Hill William*

"In *Edie & the Low-Hung Hands*, Carr's alternate world is reminiscent of Denis Johnson's *Fiskadoro*—dreamlike, haunting in its dystopian aura, and fully imagined. The humanity of his characters is never lost, despite the violence and strangeness of their existence."

—Paula Bomer, author of *Nine Months* and *Baby and Other Stories*

CPSIA information can be obtained at www.ICGtesting.com
Printed in the USA
LVOW08s0206050214

372404LV00002B/22/P

9 780984 874446